Pow

Powershell For Beginners Guide To Learning Powershell, Powershell 5 And Powershell Scripting

By

Josh Thompsons

This document is geared towards providing exact and reliable information in regards to the topic and issue covered. The publication is sold with the idea that the publisher is not required to render accounting, officially permitted, or otherwise, qualified services. If advice is necessary, legal or professional, a practiced individual in the profession should be ordered.

- From a Declaration of Principles which was accepted and approved equally by a Committee of the American Bar Association and a Committee of Publishers and Associations.

In no way is it legal to reproduce, duplicate, or transmit any part of this document in either electronic means or in printed format. Recording of this publication is strictly prohibited and any storage of this document is not allowed unless with written permission from the publisher. All rights reserved.

The information provided herein is stated to be truthful and consistent, in that any liability, in terms of inattention or otherwise, by any usage or abuse of any policies, processes, or directions contained within is the solitary and utter responsibility of the recipient reader. Under no circumstances will any legal responsibility or blame be held against the publisher for any reparation, damages, or monetary loss due to the information herein, either directly or indirectly.

Respective authors own all copyrights not held by the publisher.

The information herein is offered for informational purposes solely, and is universal as so. The presentation of the information is without contract or any type of guarantee assurance.

The trademarks that are used are without any consent, and the publication of the trademark is without permission or backing by the trademark owner. All trademarks and brands within this book are for clarifying purposes only and are the owned by the owners themselves, not affiliated with this document.

CONTENTS

Introduction

I want to thank you and congratulate you for purchasing the book, *"Powershell: Powershell For Beginners Guide To Learning Powershell, Powershell 5 And Powershell Scripting."*

This book contains proven steps and strategies on how to learn Windows PowerShell as a complete beginner.

PowerShell is an incredibly useful tool but learning it will not be a 5-minute job. It will take a certain amount of hard work and no small amount of concentration and dedication. I am going to cover just the basics here, form how to set PowerShell up to all the components that make up the tool. By the end of the book, you will have an understanding of how to use PowerShell for basic automation tasks, giving you a good grounding for increasing your knowledge to go on to bigger and better things.

Thanks again for purchasing this book, I hope you enjoy it!

Chapter 1: Let's Set Up PowerShell

The command prompt is something that most of us are familiar with, whether we have used it or not. PowerShell, on the other hand, is not quite so well-known. PowerShell is an incredibly powerful tool, much more so than the command prompt could ever hope to be and will, in time, take over from the prompt, at least on Windows systems. PowerShell provides us with a high degree of control over the operating system and with a good deal more power than we ever had before.

Let's start with a shell – what is it? The shell is nothing more than a user interface. In PowerShell, we get access to lots of different operating system services, allowing us to control more and automate a great deal of what we do. Shells can be one of two things – a command line or a full GUI – graphical user interface. Developed by Microsoft, PowerShell is designed as a way of automating some task and to help us with managing configuration on our systems. It is .NET based and it has both the command line and its own integrated scripting environment, or ISE as you will see it. The ISE is an interface that helps us to create scripts without the need for reams of commands.

Some of the tasks that PowerShell can automate are those that are time-consuming. PowerShell can be set up so that these tasks can run in the background, while you are busy on other things, without interfering with your time. You can find out which processes are not responding and stop them and we do all this by creating scripts and chaining together commands.

How to Get PowerShell

Those of you who use Windows 7, 8, 8.1 and 10 will find that PowerShell is already installed but it won't be on your desktop. Go to the built-in search bar and search for PowerShell; click on the entry in the search results – it will be the top one – and it will open. You can pin it to your taskbar or make a shortcut on your home screen for it. To do that just right click the icon and pick the option you want. Windows 10 users will find that they already have PowerShell 5, the latest version so if you are on anything earlier, you will need to upgrade it. If you are on Windows XP or Vista, you will need to install PowerShell.

Installing or Upgrading

Because PowerShell is a Windows tool, version 5 is part of

the Windows Management Framework and, for that to work, .NET framework 4.4 or higher is needed so you will need to install this before you can install PowerShell or upgrade your existing version. This only applies to those on Windows 7 or Windows Server 2008; if you are on Server 2012 or higher, .NET is already installed as part of the operating system. To see what version is installed, open your command prompt (just go to the search bar and type in command prompt) and input this command:

```
(Get-ItemProperty -Path
'HKLM:\SOFTWARE\Microsoft\NET Framework
Setup\NDP\v4\Full').Version
```

If the result of the command is "missing registry key", .NET is not installed.

Before Installing PowerShell

Don't jump to install PowerShell just for a minute because you need to be aware of a few things first.

- If you run applications such as SharePoint you need to know that the version of PowerShell you run is important because SharePoint is dependent on it. If you were to create a few scripts in SharePoint and then upgrade to a later version of PowerShell, all those scripts would break and wouldn't work

- Second, most of the code written in earlier versions of PowerShell will work on version 5.0 but the latest version is sufficiently different that problems can arise, mostly with external dependencies. These will be things like SharePoint or other software that hasn't been updated to support PowerShell 5.0.

How to Install or Upgrade to Version 5.0

The first thing you need to do is download the PowerShell installer so go to https://msdn.microsoft.com/en-us/PowerShell/wmf/5.0/requirements and download the installer that matches your specific system. Don't worry; if you do start installing the wrong installer, you will see a warning message. When the download has completed, you will be able to upgrade your system or install PowerShell 5.0 from scratch and here's how to do that:

1. Locate the installer and double click on it. You will see some on-screen instructions; follow these exactly to ensure the correct KB update is installed – it will be named Update for Windows (KBXXXXXXX).
2. PowerShell will now show up as installing under Programs and Features>PowerShell. Click to confirm the installation/upgrade, accept the EULA and then sit back and wait while the installation completes
3. Your computer will need to be rebooted so that the

installation can complete. When everything is back up and running, go to PowerShell, open it up and type the following into the console – it will show you what version you are running – this is for upgrades only. This is the command - `$PSVersionTable.PSVersion`. If the upgrade was successful, where it says Major Property, you will see the number 5.

After the Installation

When the installation is finished, the next job is to make sure that it is properly configured for running scripts. By default, scripting is disabled but you are only going to need to do the following once:

- Right-click the PowerShell icon and click on Run as Administrator to open it
- A command prompt will open in PowerShell – type this command in at the prompt - `PS> Set-ExecutionPolicy RemoteSigned`. Leave Shell open – you are going to need it again in a bit.

Now we are going to make a small edit to your profile so type this in at the command prompt:

```
PS> New-Item -Path $Profile -ItemType file -Force

PS> notepad $Profile

PS> exit
```

Now you can open PowerShell as a normal user, not as administrator.

Configuration of the Console

The console provides you with a simple way of creating your script files and running commands so you have two choices here – leave it alone and work with it as it is or configure it to how you want it. You might find that you prefer a different size of font, a new color for the background or a large bugger size. You can do all of this from the command window, adding scripts into your personal profile or by using PowerShell commands.

Configuration of the Console Properties:

The way PowerShell looks is determined solely by the settings, be they default or custom and these are in a shortcut that gets passed as an argument into PowerShell – don't worry, you will understand that a bit later on. For now, let's modify some settings:

- In the top left corner of the console window is a small PowerShell icon – click it
- Now choose Properties and 4 tabs will show up – Options, Font, Layout, and Colors

Click to make changes on each one:

- **Options** – this contains the settings for the size of the cursor and the command history. There are two options for editing – QuickEdit, which will let you use your mouse for copy/paste commands, and Insert, which will insert text in a line, rather than overwriting it
- **Font** – options for changing the style and the size of the font – these are somewhat limited though
- **Layout** – here you can pick which size buffer you want, and the size and position of the window. The buffer will set how many characters and lines are in the buffer and the window size sets how large the window is, as well as where to place it on your desktop
- **Colors** – pick which colors you want for text and background

When your changes are made, click on OK to shut the Properties box down - all of your changes are immediately applied. However, they will only stay as you see them if you open PowerShell again from the location where the changes were made, i.e. you or desktop. However, if you want those changes to be permanent, you need to do something a little different. In your text editor (Notepad for Windows), type in this and see what happens:

```
Set-Alias rc Edit-PowerShellProfile


function Prompt

{

    $mywd = (Get-Location).Path

    $mywd = $mywd.Replace( $HOME, '~' )

    Write-Host "PS " -NoNewline -ForegroundColor
DarkGreen

    Write-Host ("" + $mywd + ">") -NoNewline -
ForegroundColor Green

    return " "

}


function Edit-PowerShellProfile

{

    notepad $Profile

}
```

Save and then open up PowerShell. You should see your changes no matter where you open it from because you saved them in a profile script.

PowerShell IDE

The Integrated Development Environment, or IDE for short, is a tool that all developers and programmers choose to use. IDEs contain debuggers, code editors, and tools for build automation. There are lots of them to choose from but the best is the PowerShell integrated ISE. This is the Integrated Scripting Environment and it is a host application. It can be used to run commands from, write, test and debug your code, all from one simple graphical user interface. The PowerShell ISE has these features:

- Tab completion
- Multiline editing
- Syntax coloring
- Context-sensitive help
- Selective execution
- Support for right-to-left language

The ISE contains shortcuts to help you do many tasks that can be down in the PowerShell console. Let's say you wanted to debug a script that you wrote in the ISE, you could right-click the line and choose Toggle Breakpoint. You can also:

- Selective execution – choose to run part of your script by highlighting the section and pressing F5 or clicking on Run Script

- Multiline editing – insert blank lines under a current line in the command pane by pressing the Shift and Enter keys together
- Context sensitive help – by typing in Invoke-Item and then pressing F1, you get the help file for the Invoke_item cmdlet. You can do this with anything you want help for

There are also bits of the ISE appearance you can change and there is a profile where you can store variables, functions, commands and aliases.

Open the PowerShell ISE by:

- Clicking on Start>All Programs>Windows PowerShell>Windows PowerShell ISE

OR

- Opening PowerShell console. Open the Run box and type in CMD.exe or PowerShell_ise.exe

PowerShell Profiles

PowerShell profile scripts will run when a PowerShell session is opened. PowerShell 5.0 has support for 6 different profiles, each used for console configuration, like module loading, configuration of aliases, function definition, etc.

PowerShell console and ISE each has a profile of its own, and there are profiles for the current user and all other users. The following are the profiles and where you can find them:

1. **Current user, Current Host** - `ISE` - `$Home\[My ]Documents\WindowsPowerShell\Microsoft.P owerShellISE_profile.ps1`

2. **Current User, Current Host** - `console` - `$Home\[My ]Documents\WindowsPowerShell\Profile.ps1`

3. **Current User, All Hosts** - `$Home\[My ]Documents\Profile.ps1`

4. **All users, Current Host** - `ISE` - `$PsHome\Microsoft.PowerShellISE_profile.ps1`

5. **All Users, Current Host** - `console` - `$PsHome\Microsoft.PowerShell_profile.ps1`

6. **All Users, All Hosts** - `$PsHome\Profile.ps1`

You need to keep in mind that these profiles will move; if you can do that, you'll work just fine with all of them. When we talk of the PowerShell Profile, mostly we are talking about the Current User, Current Host

The $profile Variable

When you run a query on the $profile, an automatic variable, the path returns to the profile called Current User, Current

Host. This is the best way of having easy access to the profile path so, to make it a bit clearer, look at this script:

```
PS C:\> $profile

C:\Users\ed.IAMMRED\Documents\WindowsPowerShell\Micro
soft.PowerShell_profile.ps1

When you use the PowerShell ISE to query $profile,
you will get this output:

PS C:\Users\ed.IAMMRED> $profile

C:\Users\ed.IAMMRED\Documents\WindowsPowerShell\Micro
soft.PowerShellISE_profile.ps1
```

Don't waste time trying to work out what all that means for now; all you need to now is that there is a difference between PowerShell ISE Current User and PowerShell Console Current User – it should be obvious. It is nothing more than ISE. If you attempt to set something inside the console profile, it has to be in the ISE too.

This will all start to become clear in the following chapters.

Chapter 2: Learning the PowerShell Commands

PowerShell revolves around commands because, like the command prompt, like Python, C#, Ruby and any other computer programming language, commands are how you get PowerShell to do things. PowerShell commands are called cmdlets, pronounced command-lets, and each one is a small light script. Every cmdlet has its own function and each can perform just that function, nothing else and that makes learning PowerShell easy. Let's look at the most commonly used cmdlets:

Get-Help

Microsoft is well aware that PowerShell is something completely new for many people and, to make things easy, they included a useful command that helps you. It's called Get-Help and it does exactly what it says on the box. Used correctly, Get-Help will display help about concepts and commands in PowerShell, such as the other cmdlets, functions, workflows, aliases, scripts, CIM commands, and providers. All you need to do is type Get-help at the prompt or in the ISE and then follow it with the name of what you want help for. For example, if you wanted to know more about processes, you would type Get-help Get-Process. For a list of all the topics you can get help with, type Get-Help *.

Conceptual topics are a little different; to get help about those, the command must start with "about". For example, if you want help on comparison operators, you would type about_Comparison Operators. For a list of all the topics relating to conceptual help, just type Get-Help_* and, to see a specific topic, type Get-Help about_\<topic name>, i.e. Get-Help about_*\Comparison Operators.

For PowerShell providers, and we'll talk about these later, type Get-Help followed by the provider name. For example, if you wanted to know more about the Certificate provider you would type Get-Help Certificate.

There are shortcuts to these processes. Instead of typing in Get-Help, you could type help or man and this will display the help screens one at a time. For help on commands only, you can type \<name of cmdlet>\> -?

Get-Command

Another useful cmdlet is Get-Command, which will display a list of all the commands that can be used on your system. This will include cmdlets, aliases, scripts, functions, filters, workflows and applications. Just type get-Command * to see a list of all the commands. You will see all of those in the Path variable called $eny:path and those that are not – the latter will be shown as Application files.

For a specific command, type Get-Command and then the command name. The result will be the module that contains the command being imported and you will be able to use it immediately.

Get-Member

As with any programming language, as a beginner, the biggest issue you will face is knowing what you can and can't do when you are on the command line or writing scripts. You won't know which methods you can use, which properties and this is where Get-Member comes in. All you do is connect up to an object, pipe that object to Get-Member and you will see all the methods in the object, along with the properties, returned. For example, we already know that get-EventLog will display an object for Event Log so all you would type is Get-EventLog-List|Get-Member.

Get-ChildItem

This command is used to list all objects from the location you are in currently but there is a little more to it. For example, if we type in Get-ChildItem, you would see something like this:

```
Directory: Microsoft.Windows
PowerShell.Core\FileSystem::C:\Documents and
```

```
Settings\timdlaton



Mode                LastWriteTime
Length Name

----                -------------
------ ----

d----               3/1/2006    9:03 AM
Bluetooth Software

d---s               5/10/2006   8:55 AM          Cookies

d----               5/9/2006    2:09 PM          Desktop

d-r--               5/9/2006    8:22 AM
Favorites

d-r--               5/9/2006    2:24 PM          My
Documents

d-r--               3/1/2006    8:15 AM          Start
Menu

d---s               3/1/2006    3:41 PM
UserData

d----               3/16/2006   3:29 PM      WINDOWS
```

There really isn't a great deal to look at but the reason for that is because there were only a couple of subfolders in the location. To go further, to see the names of those subfolder and what is in each one, we need to use a parameter named recurse. This is what you would type in:

```
Get-ChildItem -recurse
```

The output will be a list of the subfolders, their names, and their contents. Later, you will learn more ways to use Get-ChildItem

Using the Format Cmdlets

PowerShell has several Format cmdlets and these give you some control over the properties for certain objects. The format cmdlets are:

- Format-Custom
- Format-List
- Format-Table
- Format-Wide

Each contains a set of default properties and these will be used if you don't make any changes. If you want a specific property displayed, use the parameter called Properties; Format-Wide will only have one property but List and Table will accept multiple property names.

.NET Objects

These are created out of .NET classes. An object is an

instance of a class, while the methods are functions that are exclusive to these objects. There is plenty of support in PowerShell for these .NET objects, providing access to static and instance methods and their properties. If you needed to call a static method on a class, you would type the name of the class in square brackets and ensure that two colons separate the class name from the method name, like this:

```
[ClassName]::MethodName(parameter list)
```

If you needed to call a method on an object, a dot would be placed in between the name of the method and the variable for the object, like this:

```
$objectReference.MethodName(parameter list)
```

.NET objects can be used to create frameworks, which allows you to only use those objects that are specifically for the tasks you are working on.

Classes Objects

A class is like a blueprint that defines the structure of an object. An object has data in it that you get to through a property and we work on those using methods. Ever since you typed your first command or cmdlet in you started working with objects.

When an object is created, you have an instance of the object and this is called instantiation. The result of this is a new object saved into memory and based on a specified class. The following example shows an object being created, derived from PSObject class – this is built-in to PowerShell and this is the way it was done before PowerShell 5.0 came along:

```
    $Properties = @{

  "FirstName" = 'Stephen"

  "LastName" = 'de Mondo'

  "WebSite" = 'www.Letslearnobjects.com'

}

$Object = New-object -TypeName psobject -Property
$properties

$Object
```

Here, we created the object and then saved into a variable named $object. Inside that variable is all the data, shown in a structured list. With version 5.0, we can now create classes ourselves and the following example shows the exact same object as the above example but, this time, in a class we created:

```
Class Author {

  $FirstName = 'Stephen"

  $LastName = 'de Mondo'
```

```
        $WebSite = 'www.Letslearnobjects.com'

}

New-Object Author
```

We can instantiate a class in two different ways:

```
#Instantiating a class method 1

    [Author]::new()

#Instantiating a class method 2

    New-Object Author
```

Both of these output identical results – method 1 uses the same syntax that we would use in C#. When PowerShell 5.0 came out in beta version, we could only use method 1 to instantiate a class.

The class shown below contains four properties:

- Vehiclemake
- Vehiclemodel
- Vehiclecolor
- VehicleType

Each property is a string and there are no predefined values in any of them:

```
Class Employee {

    [string]$Vehiclemake

    [string]$Vehiclemodel

    [string]$Vehiclecolor

    [string]$Vehicletype

}
```

The Pipeline

The best way to truly understand PowerShell is to understand the pipeline. The pipeline is one of the most important concepts in PowerShell because everything that you do in PowerShell will happen in that pipeline. To begin, consider the pipeline in a logical way – as a long length of pipe. The commands go into the pipe at one end and come out of the other end as objects. It won't always be possible to see what happens inside the pipe to change the command to the object but you can have some control over the direction it goes in. The PowerShell pipe symbol is | (a vertical bar) and this will inform PowerShell that you want the output from a command to be the input of the next command. In PowerShell, instead of passing just text, we pass objects. Let's try this out:

At the command prompt, type in Get-Service. This will create the objects that you need to represent every service that is on your system and the results will be displayed. Have a go and see what you get.

What you get are a whole load of objects, together with their properties and, to sort them into some kind of order, we use the built-in command, Sort-Object. You will need to specify the type of object that is to be sorted and PowerShell provides us with the InputObject parameter, which will accept ByValue a pipeline input. In basic terms, PowerShell will lump anything that Sort-Object detects as coming out of the pipeline in with the parameter and that means you don't need to specify the type.

To make things a little clearer, the following is a PowerShell pipeline example:

So that you get the results you want, you must use pipelined expressions. These will refine the results down to exactly what you are after and this needs to be done in a few steps, as such:

1. All processes must be sorted by Virtual Memory in descending order and to do that, we do this:

```
get-process | sort -Property "VirtualMemorySize" -
Descending
```

2. What results you get depend on whether Get-Process worked as it should. If not, you will need to make

Get-Process your first command. If you see what you expect to see, you can move on:

```
get-process | sort -Property "VirtualMemorySize" -
Descending | Select -first 10
```

3. Continue, add the steps needed until you get what you are after:

```
get-process | sort -property "VirtualMemorySize" -
descending | Select -first 10 | measure-object
VirtualMemorySize -sum -average
```

One thing you should learn from this is that objects can change and they frequently do. When we began, we had process objects but at the end, we had measurement objects. If a pipelined expression doesn't show the results you expect, try the command again and pipe the results to the Get-Member cmdlet – this will help you to identify what is coming out of the pipeline. Then, remove the last part of the expression and run it again, piping the result to Get-Member again.

Tab Complete

Another useful PowerShell feature is Tab Complete. This lets you use the tab button on your keyboard to complete lines in the script or command panes. Here's what you can do with it:

- **Complete a Command Entry:**

Go to the command or script pane and start typing in a command. Just type the first couple of letters and then press Tab. If only a single command matches, the text will be completed automatically. If there is more than one, keep pressing the Tab key until you get to the one you want and then press Enter. This can be used to complete cmdlets, parameters, variables, properties and file paths.

- **Complete a Parameter Entry for a Cmdlet**

In the command or script pane, type the cmdlet in and then add a dash (-) at the end, Press on Tab and you will see all of the parameters that go with that cmdlet. If there is only one, it will be completed automatically for you; more than one and you use the tab key to cycle through to the one you want.

That completes our chapter on PowerShell commands. Obviously, there is far more to PowerShell than what we have covered here but this does give you a good start.

Chapter 3: PowerShell Script Creation

As you start to get to grips with PowerShell, you can turn your attention to script writing. This chapter will be dedicated to showing you how to write a script, along with practical examples that you can type into your own consoles so fire up PowerShell and get ready to start scripting. First, let's just have a quick overview of what PowerShell scripting is all about:

Creating a Script and Running it

You can open a PowerShell file in the script pane and edit it directly. The file types are:

- Script files have the .ps1 extension
- Script data files have the .psd1 extension
- Script module files have the .ps1xml extension

You can open all these as well as text files, configuration files, and XML files, in the script pane.

Create a new script

Here's how to create a new script in PowerShell. Work along with this so you understand it better:

- Open PowerShell
- Select New from the toolbar or click on File>New.
- Open PowerShell Tab and click on New File – the file you just created will be there and it will have an extension of .ps1 by default.
- If you want to change that, simply rename it and save it as a different extension.

There is no limit to the number of files you can create in a PowerShell tab.

Open an Existing Script

- Click Open from the toolbar or click on File>Open
- A dialog box will appear, click the file you want to open and it will open in a new tab

Close a Script Tab

- Select the tab for the script you want to close
- Click on File>Close or on the X in the top right corner. If the file was changed since you last saved it, click on Save or Discard, depending on what you want to do.

Display a File Path

- Open the file tab and run the mouse over the name of the file – you will see the full path to the file

Run a Script

- Click File>Run or on the Run Script icon on your toolbar

Run a Section of Script

- In the script pane, highlight the part of the script that you want
- Click Run Selection on the toolbar or on File>Run Selection

Stop a Script

There are a couple of ways to do this:

- Click on File>Stop Operation or on the Stop Operation icon on the toolbar
- Press the CTRL+Break keys on the keyboard at the same time
- If no text is chosen, press on CTRL+C
- If test is chosen, CTRL+C will map that selection to

the copy function

Write and Edit Text in the Script Pane

There are several options for editing text:

- Undo or redo the last action
- Replace
- Paste
- Find
- Cut
- Copy

Enter Text to the Script Pane:

- In the script pane, click on a blank area or click View>Go to Script Pane
- Create the script

Find Text

- Click on Edit>Find in Script of press CTRL+F to find text in the script
- If the text you want is after the cursor, click Edit>Find Next in Script or press Shift+F3
- If the text is before the cursor, click Edit>Find Previous IN Script or press SHIFT+F3

Replace Text

- Click Edit>Replace in Script or press CTRL+H.
- Type the text you want to find and then the text that is to replace it
- Press Enter

Find a Line

- Press CTRL+G or click Edit>Go to Line from the script pane
- Type the number of the line you want to find

Cut Text

- Highlight the text you want to cut
- Click Edit>Cut, or click Cut on the toolbar or press CTRL+X

Paste Text

- Put the cursor where you want the text pasted
- Click Paste on the toolbar, press CTRL+V or click Edit>Paste

Indo Action

- Click Edit>Undo, press CTRL+Z or click on Undo on the toolbar

Redo Action

- Press CTRL+Y, click on Redo on the toolbar or click Edit>Redo

Saving Your Scripts

The following steps demonstrate how to name your scripts and save them. If you are working with a file that has been changed but not saved, there will be an asterisk (*) beside the name – once the file is saved, that will go.

Save

- Click Save on the toolbar, press CTRL+S or click File>Save

Save and Name

- Click File>Save As
- A dialog box will appear; in the File Name box type in the name you want to call your file
- From the Save as Type box, choose the file type

- Click Save

Save in ASCII Encoding

By default, the PowerShell ISE saves new script, script module, and script data files as Unicode but you can change this to ASCII encoding if you want. To do this we use the method for Save As on the object called $psISE.CurrentFile. Below, you can see the script for saving new scripts as .ps1 with ASCII encoding.

Windows PowerShell ISE is set, by default, to save any new script, script data or script module files as Unicode. If you wanted to save as ASCII, or any other type of encoding, use the Save As method on $psISE.CurrentFile object. The command below is used to save new scripts as MyScript.ps1 but with ASCII encoding:

```
$psise.CurrentFile.SaveAs("MyScript.ps1",
[System.Text.Encoding]::ASCII)
```

Next, you can see how to replace current files with files that have the same name and ASCII encoding:

```
$psise.CurrentFile.Save([System.Text.Encoding]::ASCII
)
```

The following command shows what your current file is encoded in:

```
$psise.CurrentFile.encoding
```

PowerShell Script Files

Open your PowerShell ISE and type the examples in this section in – ensure that you start on line 1 so that everything works as it should do.

A PowerShell script file is just a text file with a file extension of .ps1. It is not a command batch file and it isn't going to run in quite the same way that you run the commands yourself. Let me make that a little clearer for you. Open your console window and type the following command in; run them and don't forget to press the enter key after you input each line of code and don't forget to start on line 1.

```
Get-Service
```

```
Get-Process
```

Type them into the script editing pane in ISE and run them. Each will provide its own result. When you hit the Enter key in PowerShell, a new pipeline is started and whatever you type on the line will go into the new pipeline. PowerShell converts it to text at the end. If you run both of those commands in a normal console, you get two pipelines; in ISE they will both go into a single pipeline, as such:

```
Get-Service; Get-Process
```

You should get pretty much the same result as you got when the script was run.

What I am trying to show you is that scripts are only supposed to produce on output type; the absolute last thing you need is for one script to show multiple command types into a single pipeline simultaneously. That should be a rule of thumb – it will only be different when a script is being used for multiple functions; in this case, each function will have its own output type.

Variables

If you have any experience with computer programming, you will know that a variable is nothing more than a storage place, where you can store all sorts of things. The storage place is named – there are naming conventions to follow when you do this, namely only using underscores (_) and the letters a to z or A to Z, and the numbers 0 to 9. The name you provide will reference the storage place as a whole but, if you wanted that reference to point towards the contents of the storage place, you would prefix the name with a $. That 4 will not be a part of the name; it is just to show PowerShell that all you want is what is in the storage place, not the place itself. Have a look at the following examples:

```
$var = 'hello'
```

```
$number = 1
```

```
$numbers = 1,2,3,4,5,6,7,8,9
```

The above shows you the assignment operator (=) and how to use it to place items into a variable. The final example will result in an array and the reason for this is because each item is separated with a comma. Any list of items that is separated in this way is called an array or a collection. The first example shows how to assign a string object; the characters you see in the quote marks are the characters in the string.

As a beginner, you may find it confusing that PowerShell doesn't understand variable meanings. For example, a variable with the name of $computername won't tell PowerShell that the variable contains a computer name. By the same token, $numbers won't tell PowerShell that the variable contains more than a single number. In short, it doesn't matter with you use singular or plural for your variable names. Try this example:

```
$numbers = 1
```

This code is just as valid as the one below:

```
$numbers = 'bob.'
```

When a variable contains several values, we need to use a specific syntax if you just want to access a single value:

- $numbers[0] is the first,

- $numbers[1] is the second,

- $numbers[-1] is the last,

- $numbers[-2] is the second-last and so on.

Quotation Marks

To delimit a variable, you should always use single quote marks. The only times you should need to use double quotes are:

1. When the variable contents have been inserted into a string. When the double quotes are used, PowerShell will look for $ and it will assume that everything that follows $, up to the first instance of an illegal character, will be the name of a variable. The contents of the variable will then go in place of $ and the name of the variable. For example:

```
$name = Simon

$prompt = "My name is $name"
```

$prompt will now be named as "My name is Simon" because $name was replaced with the variable contents. This is a great way of joining to strings together without using concatenation.

2. When you use an escape character, backtick or grave accent. PowerShell looks inside the double quotes to see if these are present and will do whatever is required. Try these examples:

```
$debug = "`$computer contains $computer"

$head = "Column`tColumn`tColumn"
```

In the first example, the first $ has been escaped and that takes the special meaning away; the special meaning is that $ is a variable accessor.

In the second example, `t represents the horizontal tab. PowerShell will place one tab on each column

3. When you need to use single quotes within a string:

```
$filter1 = "name='BITS'"

$computer = 'BITS'

$filter2 = "name='$computer'"
```

The literal string has a name of name=BITS and you note that the entire name is inside double quotes. $filter1 and $filter2 now have the same but $filter2 made the journey in a different way, with the double quotes. Note – the only quotes that count to PowerShell are the outermost quotes;

every other one will be ignored.

Object Members and Variables

Everything that is in PowerShell is an object, right down to
the most basic of strings. You can pipe any object to the
cmdlet called Get-Member to display the object type name
and any members of the object, including any methods and
their properties:

```
$var = 'Hello'

$var | Get-Member
```

If you don't need PowerShell to access an entire object within
a variable, you need to insert a period (.) after the variable
name. This will tell PowerShell that you only need to access a
single method or a single property. After the period (.) insert
the name of the specific method or property.

Method names always have to be followed by a set of
parentheses. If a method will accept input arguments, those
arguments must be specified inside the parentheses and, if
there is more than one, they must be listed with a comma
between each one. Not all methods need arguments but you
must still use the parentheses; just leave them empty:

```
$svc = Get-Service
```

```
$svc[0].name

$name = $svc[1].name

$name.length

$name.ToUpper()
```

Note that, on the second line PowerShell is accessing the first item that is in $svc. The period (.) tells PowerShell that only one property or method is to be accessed and then tells PowerShell which one – in this example, it is the property called name. Line 5 indicates accessing a method by inserting the name following the period (.) and then ending with the parentheses.

Normally, the period is considered as an illegal character in variable names and, as a result, line 2 in the next example will not work how you expect it to:

```
$service = 'bits'

$name = "Service is $service.ToUpper()"

$upper = $name.ToUpper()

$name = "Service is $upper"
```

On line 2, note that $name has got "Service is BITS.ToUPPER()" while, on line 4, $name has got "Service is BITS."

Parentheses

We know that parentheses must be used with the methods of
an object but they are also to use as a way of telling
PowerShell what order to execute the statements. In other
words, if something is inside parentheses, PowerShell knows
that it has to be executed first. The expression between the
parentheses will be replaced with the expression result. Have
a look at this example and try it for yourself; see if you can
understand it:

```
$name = (Get-Service)[0].name

Get-Service -computerName (Get-Content names.txt)
```

On line 1, you can see that $name has the name that goes
with the first service on your system. To read this properly,
begin with the expression between the parentheses – this is
where PowerShell will start Get-Service will resolve to an
array of services and the [0] access the initial item within the
array. That is followed by the period (.) so we know that a
method or a property is going to be accessed and not the
entire object. Lastly, we have the service name.

On line 2, the expression between the parentheses will read
the contents of a text file. If there is one computer name to
one line, Get-Content will return an array of the names.
These are then passed to Get-Service, to the "-
computerName" parameter and, because this parameter may

take string arrays, any parenthetical expression (an expression inside parentheses) that is able to return a string array can be passed to the parameter.

PowerShell Scripting Language

In comparison to other programming languages, PowerShell is simple, with no more than 24 keywords in it. That said, it is more than man enough for the job it needs to do and, while I can't possibly take you through everything, I am going to cover the main constructs. Don't forget; if you want help, use "about ..." for a specific topic or "about***" for a list of all conceptual help topics.

- **The If Construct**

The if construct is used for decision-making and it looks something like this:

```
If ($this -eq $that) {

   # commands

} elseif ($those -ne $them) {

   # commands

} elseif ($we -gt $they) {

   # commands

} else {
```

```
# commands

}
```

It is mandatory to include the if keyword in this construct, followed by an expression within parentheses. This expression must have a value of either True or False. PowerShell will interpret any non-zero value as True and any zero value as False.

PowerShell also knows the built-in variables called $true and $false, as representative of Boolean values. If the parenthetical expression evaluates to True, the commands within the curly brackets get executed. If the evaluation is False, the command will not be executed.

- **The elseif Construct**

The elseif construct will work in the same way; it has its own expression inside a set of parentheses and it has to evaluate as True or False. The else block can only be executed if none of the blocks that come before it executes.

# denotes a comment. Comments are purely to make notes about the code and PowerShell will not take any notice of anything that comes after the comment character up tot eh carriage return. Note, in the above example, that the constructs were formatted very carefully. You may also see something similar to this:

```
if ($those -eq $these)
```

```
{

    #commands

}
```

It isn't important where the curly brackets go, all that
matters is that you are consistent in your placement. The
same works for indentation. Every line that is within a set of
curly brackets must be indented exactly the same and the
easy way to do this is to use the Tab key, which indents to 4
spaces by default. Indentation is one of the core practices in
any programming language and is something you need to get
into the habit of doing. If you don't, when you get to more
complicated scripts, your curly brackets simply won't match.
Look at the following example of a poorly formatted script:

```
function mine {

if ($this -eq $that){

get-service

}}
```

Note how difficult it is to read. It is also harder to maintain,
to find problems in it and to debug it. You don't need to add
the space after the parentheses but you will find the code
much easier to read, as you can see from the next example:

```
function mine {

  if ($this -eq $that){
```

```
get-service

 }

}
```

That last parenthesis, the closing one, doesn't need to be
alone but it does neaten the code up. If you learn how to
format your code properly and tidily, you will find scripting
so much easier.

- **The Do While Construct**

The do while construct is a looping construct and we use it
when we want command blocks repeated, provided a
condition evaluates to True or until it evaluates to True.
Have a look at this example:

```
Do {

  # commands

} While ($this -eq $that)
```

The commands that are contained in the curly brackets will
be executed at least once and the while condition will not be
evaluated until after the first command execution. If you
move the while condition, the commands are only going to
execute if the condition starts off as being True. Look at
another example:

```
While (Test-Path $path) {

  # commands
```

}

There is no comparison operator in this example and the reason for this is that the Test-Path cmdlet already returns a value of True or False so there is nothing to compare it with.

The expression inside the parentheses in a construct only needs to do one thing: it must simplify to either True or to False. If Test-path is used, or you use another command that defaults to True or False, you don't need to use anything else.

- **The ForEach Construct**

This is similar to the ForEach cmdlet, with the only difference being the syntax used, The ForEach construct is used to enumerate objects inside a specified array, allowing you to work with them on an individual basis:

```
$services = Get-Service

ForEach ($service in $services) {

  $service.Stop()

}
```

Don't think too hard about this. All you need to keep in your mind is that plurals don't means anything to PowerShell. The name is there just to tell you that there is at least one service in it, that's all.

On the second line, you can see the keyword, in. This is part of the ForEach syntax and the variable called $service is nothing more than a fictional name.

PowerShell will repeat commands that are inside the curly brackets, or the construct, once for every object contained in the 2nd variable. On each repeat, one object is removed from the second variable and placed into the first variable until all of the objects are used.

Other Constructs

These are the most important constructs you can use in PowerShell but there are more. Use the built-in topics to get the information you want about any of them.

Sometimes, you can use the constructs we talked about above to replace one or more of the other ones. For example, an if construct could be used with multiple elif sections instead of using Switch. Or, you could use a ForEach-Object cmdlet or a ForEach construct instead of using For. An example of that would be a script that had a loop that you needed to execute a total of 10 times:

```
1..10 | ForEach-Object -process {

    # the code is going to repeat 10 times

    # use $_ to access the current iteration

    # number
```

```
}
```

What it boils down to is picking the right construct to do the job.

Functions

Functions are a special type of construct and they contain groups of related commands that will all perform a specific job. Generally, you would take a PowerShell script and wrap a function around it, like this:

```
function Mine {

   Get-Service

   Get-Process

}

Mine
```

On line 5, you can see that we have defined a new function and turned Mine into a command. Now you can enter the name when you want the function to run; that is what is going on in line 5. Functions tend to be contained in script files and you can have multiple functions in one script. It is even possible to have a function inside of another function.

Adding Parameters to a Script

It isn't very likely that you will create a script that will
perform the same way every time it is run. Most of the time,
scripts will have variable data or behaviors in them and these
are helped with the use of parameters.

A parameter must always be defined first, at the very top of a
script. These can be defined in specific ways and each
definition may have a comment before it but the parameter
itself must always be the first piece of code or first line
executed. The parameters are separated by commas and it is
more helpful if each one can go on its own line, like this:

```
param (

    [string]$computername,

    [string]$logfile,

    [int]$attemptcount = 5

)
```

In this example, we have defined 3 parameters. Each is used
the same way as a variable inside the script. Look on line 4l
we have assigned a default value to the variable called
$attemptcount. Any input parameters will automatically
override the defaults but, if there is no parameter specified at
the time the script runs, the defaults will be used. The next
example shows several ways a script can run – we have saved

this as Test.ps1:

```
./test -computername SERVER

./test -comp SERVER -log err.txt -attempt 2

./test SERVER err.txt 2

./test SERVER 2

./test -log err.txt -attempt 2 -comp SERVER
```

The script will accept the parameters in the same way that a cmdlet accepts parameters. The parameter names are variable names with the addition of the dash that precedes a parameter. Here's how the above code works:

- In line 1, we have specified a single parameter. $logfile contains nothing and $attemptcount has the default value of 5
- In line 2, we have specified three parameters using shortened names
- In line 3, the parameters are all positionally displayed without names – remember that you must provide the correct values in the correct order
- In line 4 is an example of what happens if you are not careful. $computername has got SERVER in it and $logfile has 2 in it. $attemptcount still has 5 and this is not what was meant to happen. This is the result of not using parameter names
- In line 5 we can see it all looks so much better. While

we haven't specified the parameters in order, we have used names.

Hopefully, this all means something to you. I would suggest that you repeat this chapter as many times as necessary to understand all the concepts discussed and practice all the examples given.

Chapter 4: PowerShell Providers

Earlier we mentioned providers, now it's time to introduce you to them. A PowerShell provider lets you look at your stored data in the same way that you can look at files in your file system. For example, one of the built-in providers is called the Registry provider and it helps you to go through the registry just like you would look through the files on your hard drive. There are also providers that let you override any of the Item cmdlets, like Get-Item or Set-Item, in a way that allows you to treat stored data like you would treat directories and the files in them when you navigate a file system.

Basically, a PowerShell provider gives you a logical way of accessing and working through the data stores and editing what is in them. The drive defines the point at which you enter the data store and this will be of a provider-defined type. For example, using the Registry provider, you can gain access to the hives and the keys in the registry, and the drives, HKLM and HKCU, would define the hives that you are accessing.

When you write a provider, you must specify the drives that are created automatically when the provider is available, the default drives, in other words. You will also define any methods that are used in creating new drives which can use that provider.

Provider Types

PowerShell contains several provider types, and each will have a different level of function. These are implemented in a class that is created from descendants of the class called cmdletProvider.

Provider Cmdlets

A provider cmdlet can implement any method that compares to specific cmdlets. It can create behaviors for each of the cmdlets to determine how it will work in drives for the specific provider. There are a number of cmdlet sets available and these will depend on the type of the provider.

Provider Paths

Given that you are able to work through a provider drive in the same way that you would work through a file system, it wouldn't be wrong of you to expect the provider path syntax to be the same as the paths used when navigating files. When a provider cmdlet is run, you must state which path the item will be accessed from and that path is then interpreted in one of several ways. Every provider must support one or more of these path types:

- **Drive-Qualified**

A drive-qualified path is made up of a combination of:

   o   The item name
   o   The container and the sub container where the item is
   o   The PowerShell drive used to access the item

The drive itself will be defined by the provider and the path must start with the drive name and a colon, i.e. get-childitem c:

- **Provider-Qualified**

Every provider has to have support for provider-qualified paths, so that PowerShell can initialize the provider and then un-initialize it. For example, if you use the FileSystem provider, it can be initialized and un-initialized because it has the following provider-qualified path -

```
FileSystem::\\uncshare\abc\bar
```

- **Provider-Direct**

For you to access the PowerShell providers remotely, the provider needs support for provider-direct paths; these pass from the current location directly to the provider. For example, the provider-direct path of the Registry provider is `\\server\regkeypath`

- **Provider-Internal**

PowerShell providers need to provide support for provider-internal paths so that the provider cmdlet can get to data through an Application Programming Interface or API. You will see this in the provider-qualified class, following the double colon (::). For example, in the FileSystem provider, you will see a provider-internal path that reads `\\uncshare\abc\bar`.

Dynamic Parameters

PowerShell providers have the ability to define dynamic parameters. These are used in provider cmdlets when a value has been specified for a static parameter of that cmdlet. The provider does this through the implementation of one or more method for dynamic parameters.

Provider Capabilities

These are features that the provider either implements or supports, including the use of wildcards, support for transactions and the ability to filter items. These capabilities are specified when the provider class definition is decorated with the cmdletProvider attribute. For example, this is the attribute you will see in the Registry provider -

```
[CmdletProvider(RegistryProvider.ProviderName,
ProviderCapabilities.ShouldProcess |
ProviderCapabilities.Transactions)]
```

The first parameter is giving the name of the provider and the second one specifies which capabilities are to be used. In this example, the Registry provider is supporting a call to the ShouldProcess method and this lets the provider confirm actions before performing them, and also support transactions.

Provider Cmdlet Help

When you write a provider, you are able to implement Help for each of the provider cmdlets that are supported. The Help is in the format of a Help topic for the individual cmdlets or multiple versions for those cmdlets that have different actions, depending on what the dynamic parameter does. PowerShell displays these Help topics using the GetHelpMaml method. The PowerShell engine supplies the name of the user-specified cmdlet, along with the current user path. This path is required only if multiple versions of the provider cmdlet are implemented for different drives.

The GetHelpMaml method should return a string with the cmdlet Help XML.

The Help file content follows the schema for writing the standalone cmdlet Help files, in that it uses PSMAML XML. To add content into the Provider help file for the custom cmdlet, you write it into the CmdletHelpPath element. Look at the following example, showing the command element for a cmdlet that relates to a single provider and how the provider cmdlet name should be specified:

<CmdletHelpPaths>

  <command:command>

  <command:details>

<command:name>ProviderCmdletName</command:name>

    <command:verb>Verb</command:verb>

    <command:noun>Noun</command:noun>

  <command:details>

  </command:command>

<CmdletHelpPath>

The File System

PowerShell FileSystem providers let you work on directories and files in the following ways

- Change
- Add
- Delete
- Clear

You will be able to see the drives that correspond to your computer drives, including any that are mapped to networks. As such, all the drives can be referenced from within PowerShell and you can refer to your files, folders and directories the same as you would in your operating system.

In order to refer to a specific drive, you must first specify the drive name and then add a colon. This provider is not case sensitive so you don't need to worry about whether to use c: or C: to access C drive. To ensure that the drive name is qualified, follow this format:

- The drive name
- A colon
- Directory and/or subdirectory names
- The name of the file, if required

Each of these elements needs a forward or backward slash to separate them – chose one and stick to it, don't mix \ and/ in the same path! The next example is the path of Shell.dll, a

file on C: located in the Windows directory in system32
subdirectory:

```
C:\Windows\System32\shell.dll
```

If spaces are to be included in any part of a qualified name,
the entire name must be inside double quotes, as such:

```
"C:\Program Files\Internet Explorer\iexplore.exe"
```

The period (.) is representative of the current location of the
file system. For example, if the current location was
C:\Windows\System32, the Shell.dll file in the directory
would be referred to as:

```
.\Shell.dll
```

If you want to view and manage your files and folders with
the FileSystem provider, you would need to use the specific
provider cmdlets, such as Set-Location or Get-ChildItem.
There is also a mkdir function in PowerShell that uses the
cmdlet called New-Item to help you create a new directory.

The Alias

The Alias provider gives you the following abilities with
PowerShell aliases:

- Add
- Get
- Clear

- Change
- Delete

An alias is another name for an executable file, a cmdlet or a function and, although there are a certain number of aliases built-in to PowerShell you can add your own, either to your profile or to the current session.

You will only find alias objects in the Alias provider and it is nothing more than a flat namespace with no child items. Each object is an instance of the following class:

```
System.Management.Automation.AliasInfo.
```

You can find the data store of the provider in Alias: drive. To work with aliases, use this command to change locations to the Alias: drive:

```
Set-Location alias:
```

If you want to work from other drives in PowerShell, you add the name of the Alias: drive to the path when referencing it from elsewhere.

There are a certain number of cmdlets in PowerShell that let you view or change aliases:

- Export-Alias
- Get-Alias
- Import-Alias
- New-Alias

- Set-Alias

When you use these cmdlets, you do not need to use Alias: drive.

The Function

The Function provider gives you the following abilities with PowerShell functions:

- Add
- Change
- Delete
- Clear

Functions are blocks of code with names and each performs a unique action. When you type in a function name, the code in the function runs. Filters are blocks of code with names, each responsible for specific conditions for specific actions. You can input a filter name instead of a condition, like you do in the Where-Object command.

In the Function: drive the names of the functions are preceded by the label, "function: and the filters are preceded by the label, "filter". Regardless of these labels, they will operate exactly as they are meant to provided they are used in the correct context.

The Function provider only has function and filter objects,

with no child items, and is a flat namespace. Functions are instances of the following class:

```
System.Management.Automation.FunctionInfo
```

And filters are instances of the following class:

```
System.Management.Automation.FilterInfo.
```

The Function provider data store is in Function: drive; to work with them, use Set_Location Function: to change your location to Function: drive. To reference them from elsewhere, add Function: name to the path.

The Function provider supports the cmdlets that contain Item in the name, except for the one called Invoke-Item. It will also support Get-Content and Set-Content. There is no support for the cmdlets that contain the ItemProperty noun or for nay cmdlets with the Filter parameter.

Changes that are made to function will only have an effect on the current console. To save changes permanently, add the specific function to the profile or save the current console by using Export-Console.

The Environment

The Environment provider lets you do the following to the PowerShell environment variables:

- Change
- Add
- Get
- Delete
- Clear

The provider only has objects that represent the environment variables, no child items, and is a flat namespace.

The environment variables are instances of the following class:

```
System.Collections.DictionaryEntry.
```

The dictionary key is the name of the variable and the dictionary value is the value of the variable.

The Environment provider data store is in the Env: drive. To work with them, use Set-location Env: to change your location to the Env: drive and, to work with them from elsewhere, use Env: drive in the path.

Environment provider supports all Item cmdlets, except for Invoke-Item, and also the Get-Content and Set-Content cmdlets. It does not support any ItemProperty cmdlets to the Filter parameter in any cmdlets.

The names of the environment variables follow the naming conventions for normal variables and you cannot use = in the name. Any changes that are made to variables will only affect your current session; to save them, add them to the profile or use Export-Console to save your current session.

The Registry

The Registry provider lets you do the following to entries, keys, and values in the Registry:

- Add
- Get
- Change
- Delete
- Clear

Keys are instances of the Microsoft.win32.RegistryKey class and the entries are instances of the PSCustomObject class.

Through the Registry provider, you can access a hierarchical namespace consisting of keys and osubkeys. You won't find any of the values or entries in the hierarchy because they are the properties of the individual keys.

The Registry provider supports all Item cmdlets except for Invoke-Item, and these should be used when you work with keys and subkeys from the registry. The provider also support the ItemProperty cmdlets, always to be used when working with registry entries. There is no support for any

Content cmdlet.

Each key in the registry is protected by security descriptors and these can be seen with Get-Acl.

The Certificate

The Certificate provider lets you see certificates and certificate stores in the Certificate namespace. It can also be used as a way of opening the Certificates Snapin for Microsoft Management Console (MMC).

It is worth noting that, for any version of PowerShell after 3.0, the location of the Certificate provider, Microsoft.PowerShell.Security module, is not imported into each session automatically. Instead, you must use Cert: drive together with the Import-Module cmdlet or a command that uses Cert: drive, i.e. Set-Location Cert:

PowerShell versions 3, 4, and 5 also provide much better SSL management support for the Certificate provider. SSL is otherwise known as Secure Socket Layer and support is for the web hosting certificates. This support is provided through dynamic parameter support along with cmdlets that can create and delete the certificate stores in LocalMachine and the cmdlets that find, move and delete certificates.

The Get-ChildItem cmdlet in Cert also has some new

dynamic parameters:

- SSLServerAuthentication

- ExpiringInDays

- EKU

- DnsName

DeleteKey is a brand-new dynamic parameter that can be found in Remove-Item in Cert:

All of these parameters are in PowerShell 3 or higher and work on Windows server 2012 and above and on IIS 8.0.

The object named X509Certificate 2 has a few new script properties:

- SendAsTrustedIssuer

- EnhancedKeyUsageList

- DnsNameList

All of these are used to make it easy to find certificates and manage them.

If that wasn't enough to take in, there are also now cmdlets in Microsoft.PowerShell.Security module that get certificates, get Authenticode signatures and set those signatures. An easy way to see what cmdlets are in that module is just to type in Get-Command -module *security.

Chapter 5: Working with Files and Folders

Think back to how you navigate your way through the file system on your hard drive; you can do the same with drives on PowerShell and we're going to look at manipulating items:

How to List The Contents of a Folder

To see all the content of a folder, use the Get-ChildItem cmdlet. Adding a Force parameter will show you the hidden and the system items. The following command displays the Powershell Drive: C contents – try it yourself and you will see it contains exactly what your C: on your hard drive contains.

```
Get-ChildItem -Force C:\
```

This command lists the items that are directly contained in the drive. If you want to see more, like everything inside the direct items, you would need to add the -Recurse parameter to your command. However, depending on what is stored on your computer, this can take some time to execute:

```
Get-ChildItem -Force C:\ -Recurse
```

Get-ChildItem uses built-in parameters, like Filter, Exclude, Path and Include, to filter items but this tends to be done on Name. If you want to go deeper with filtering you can use Where-Object. The next example shows all executable drives contained on C; inside the Program Files folder, modified after 1st December 2016 and from 1 to 10 MB in size:

```
Get-ChildItem -Path $env:ProgramFiles -Recurse -
Include *.exe | Where-Object -FilterScript
{($_.LastWriteTime -gt "2016-12-01") -and ($_.Length
-ge 1m) -and ($_.Length -le 10m)}
```

How to Copy Files and Folders

If you want to copy a file or a folder, use the cmdlet called Copy-Item. The next example shows how to back the contents of C:\ boot.ini to C:\boot.bak:

```
Copy-Item -Path c:\boot.ini -Destination c:\boot.bak
```

If that destination already exists, the copy will not wor. To overwrite an existing destination, you need to use the Force parameter:

```
Copy-Item -Path c:\boot.ini -Destination c:\boot.bak
-Force
```

This works on all destinations, even read-only ones.

It is pretty much the same when you want to copy a folder. The next command copies C:\tempztest1 to a new location folder, C:\temp\DeleteMe – this si done recursively:

```
Copy-Item C:\temp\test1 -Recurse c:\temp\DeleteMe
```

You can also select items that you want to copy, This command copies all .txt files from C:\data over to C:\temp\text:

```
Copy-Item -Filter *.txt -Path c:\data -Recurse -
Destination c:\temp\text
```

You can use other tools for copying items from the file system. Objects like Com, XCOPY, and ROBOCOPY will work in PowerShell, for example, using a COM class called Scripting.FileSystem to back up C:\boot.ino to C:\boot.bak, like this:

```
(New-Object -ComObject
Scripting.FileSystemObject).CopyFile("c:\boot.ini",
"c:\boot.bak")
```

How to Create New Files and Folders

It doesn't matter which of the Providers you use, it is the same process to create a new folder or file. If there are two or more item types in the Provider, like FileSystem, for example, which is able to tell the difference between a file and folder, you must specify the item type you want. This next command creates a new folder, C:\temp\New Folder:

```
New-Item -Path 'C:\temp\New Folder' -ItemType
"directory"
```

This command creates a new empty file, C:\temp\New Folder\file.txt:

```
New-Item -Path 'C:\temp\New Folder\file.txt' -
ItemType "file"
```

How to Remove All Files and Folders from a Folder

You can remove items using the cmdlet called Remove-Item. However, if that item has other items inside it, you must first confirm that you want to remove it. For example, attempting to delete C:\temp.DeleteMe would result in PowerShell asking you to confirm it first because it has other items inside it:

```
Remove-Item C:\temp\DeleteMe

Confirm

The item at C:\temp\DeleteMe has children and the -
recurse parameter was not

specified. If you continue, all children will be
removed with the item. Are you

sure you want to continue?

[Y] Yes  [A] Yes to All  [N] No  [L] No to All  [S]
```

```
Suspend   [?] Help

(default is "Y"):
```

If you definitely want to delete everything, and you don't need confirmation prompts for every item contained in the main item, you must use the recursive parameter:

```
Remove-Item C:\temp\DeleteMe -Recurse
```

How to Map Local Folders as Windows Accessible Drives

You can also map local folders by using the subst command. This next example shows you how to create a local drive called P: rooted in the local directory, Program Files:

```
subst p: $env:programfiles
```

In the same way that they do with network drives, any drive mapped in PowerShell, using that command, will be visible to the Shell straight away.

How to Read Text Files into Arrays

Storage of data is done in many ways but perhaps the most common format is a file with separate lines, each one an individual element. To read the entire file, we use the cmdlet called Get-Content, like this:

```
PS> Get-Content -Path C:\boot.ini

[boot loader]
```

```
timeout=5

default=multi(0)disk(0)rdisk(0)partition(1)\WINDOWS

[operating systems]

multi(0)disk(0)rdisk(0)partition(1)\WINDOWS="Microsof
t Windows XP Professional"

 /noexecute=AlwaysOff /fastdetect

multi(0)disk(0)rdisk(0)partition(1)\WINDOWS="
Microsoft Windows XP Professional

with Data Execution Prevention" /noexecute=optin
/fastdetect
```

This cmdlet treats any data that is read as an array, keeping one element on one line. You can confirm that this has been done by checking the length of the returned content:

```
PS> (Get-Content -Path C:\boot.ini).Length

6
```

This is an incredibly useful command to use when you want to add lists of information directly into PowerShell, for example, if you wanted to store lists of computer names or IP addresses in a file named C:\temp\domainMembers.txt, wth each name or IP address son a separate line. The contents can then be retrieved with the Get-Content cmdlet and you can put them into a variable named $computers.

```
$Computers = Get-Content -Path
```

```
C:\temp\DomainMembers.txt
```

What we have no is an array, with each name as an element, and that array is called $Computers.

Output to HTML

To convert a .NET Framework object into HTML, so you can display it on a webpage, you would use the cmdlet called ConvertTo-HTML. This will display the output of a command on a web page and the parameters of that cmdlet can be used to:

- Select the properties of objects
- Specify the format of a table
- Specify the format of a list
- Specify the HTML page file
- To insert text before an object, after an object or both
- To return a list fragment or a table and not a strict DTD page

When you submit multiple objects to the ConvertTo-Html cmdlet, PowerShell automatically creates a table or a list that is based on the properties from the first object. If the other objects don't have any of the specified properties, there will be an empty cell as the property value of the object. If there are any additional properties in the rest of the objects, the property value will be excluded from the file. Have a look at these examples:

Example 1

Create a web page that will show the current date:

```
PS C:\> ConvertTo-Html -InputObject (Get-Date)
```

This creates a page in HTML that shows the properties of the current date. We used the InputObject parameter to pass the results of the Get-Date command t the ConvertTo-Html cmdlet.

Example 2

Create a web page that shows the PowerShell Aliases:

```
PS C:\> Get-Alias | ConvertTo-Html > aliases.htm

PS C:\> Invoke-Item aliases.htm
```

This creates a page in HTML that lists the Aliases from the current console. We use the cmdlet called Get-Alias to get the aliases and we use the pipeline operator to pass the aliases to the ConvertTo-Html cmdlet. This then creates the page in HTML.

Output to XML

The ConvertTo-XML cmdlet will create representations of at least one object of the .NET Framework, which will be XML-based. To use this cmdlet, an object has to be piped to it and you use the InputObject parameter to specify the object.

When you pipe multiple objects to ConvertTo-XML or you use InputObject to submit multiple objects, ConvertTo-XML returns a single XML document containing a list of all object representations.

This cmdlet is like the Export-Clixml cmdlet with the exception that the latter stores the XMLs in a file while the former returns the XML, allowing you to continue working on it. Look at these examples:

Example 1:

Convert a date to XML

```
PS C:\> Get-Date | ConvertTo-Xml
```

The command converts the current date, an object of type DateTime, into XML

Example 2:

Convert a process to XML

```
PS C:\> ConvertTo-Xml -As "Document" -InputObject
(Get-Process) -Depth 3
```

The command converts a process object into a document of
XML type. A process object represents the processes that
happen on your computer.

Working with CSV Files

A CSV file is a simple file format that contains data in tabular
form. Excel is an example of CSV. You can work with these
files in 2 ways:

- **Export or Convert**

The cmdlet called ConvertTo-CSV returns a series of strings,
each one with a comma separating each from the next. These
strings represent objects. Next, you would use ConvertFrom-
CSV to recreate each of the objects from the strings. The
resulting objects will be CSV versions of the originals and
will have no methods in them. However, they will contain a
string representation of each property value.

To convert objects to CSV strings, you can also use these
cmdlets: T: Microsoft.PowerShell.Commands.Export-CSV
and T: Microsoft.PowerShell.Commands.Import-CSV. There
is just one difference between Export-CSV and ConvertTo-
CSV and that is that the latter saves the strings to a file.

The ConvertTo-CSV parameters are used to specify delimiters other than commas or to inform ConvertTo-CSV that the delimiter that should be used in the current culture is the default one.

Example 1

```
PS C:\> get-process powershell | convertto-csv

#TYPE System.Diagnostics.Process

"__NounName","Name","Handles","VM","WS","PM","NPM","P
ath","Company","CPU","FileVersion","ProductVersion","
Description",

"Product","BasePriority","ExitCode","HasExited","Exit
Time","Handle","HandleCount","Id","MachineName","Main
WindowHandle"

,"MainWindowTitle","MainModule","MaxWorkingSet","MinW
orkingSet","Modules","NonpagedSystemMemorySize","Nonp
agedSystemMem

orySize64","PagedMemorySize","PagedMemorySize64","Pag
edSystemMemorySize","PagedSystemMemorySize64","PeakPa
gedMemorySize

","PeakPagedMemorySize64","PeakWorkingSet","PeakWorki
ngSet64","PeakVirtualMemorySize","PeakVirtualMemorySi
ze64","Priori

tyBoostEnabled","PriorityClass","PrivateMemorySize","
```

PrivateMemorySize64","PrivilegedProcessorTime","Proce
ssName","Proc

essorAffinity","Responding","SessionId","StartInfo","
StartTime","SynchronizingObject","Threads","TotalProc
essorTime","U

serProcessorTime","VirtualMemorySize","VirtualMemoryS
ize64","EnableRaisingEvents","StandardInput","Standar
dOutput","Sta

ndardError","WorkingSet","WorkingSet64","Site","Conta
iner"

"Process","powershell","216","597544960","60399616","
63197184","21692","C:\WINDOWS\system32\WindowsPowerSh
ell\v1.0\powe

rshell.exe","Microsoft
Corporation","3.4788223","6.1.6587.1
(fbl_srv_powershell(nigels).070711-
0102)","6.1.6587.1","Win

dows PowerShell","Microsoft® Windows® Operating
System","8",,"False",,"860","216","5132",".","5636936
","Windows PowerSh

ell 2.0 (04/17/2008
00:10:40)","System.Diagnostics.ProcessModule
(powershell.exe)","1413120","204800","System.Diagnost
i

cs.ProcessModuleCollection","21692","21692","63197184
","63197184","320080","320080","63868928","63868928",
"60715008","6

```
0715008","598642688","598642688","True","Normal","631
97184","63197184","00:00:00.2028013","powershell","15
","True","1",

"System.Diagnostics.ProcessStartInfo","4/21/2008
3:49:19
PM",,"System.Diagnostics.ProcessThreadCollection","00
:00:03.51

00225","00:00:03.3072212","597544960","597544960","Fa
lse",,,,"60399616","60399616",,
```

This is a rather unwieldy and long command that converts a process object to CSV format, using Get-Process to place the PowerShell process on the local system. The pipeline operator is then used to pass the command to ConvertTo-CSV, where it is converted to a string array, with each item separated by a comma.

Example 2

```
PS C:\> $date = get-date

PS C:\> convertto-csv -inputobject $date -delimiter
";" -notypeinformation
```

This convers date objects into CSV.

In the first example, Get-Date was used to get the date and save it in the $date variable. In the second example, ConvertTo-CSV was used to convert the DateTime object that was in $date to CSV format. This command used the parameter called InputObject to specify which object is to be converted and the Delimiter parameter to specify which delimiter needs to be used to separate the properties. Lastly, the NoTypeInformation parameter suppresses the #TYPE string.

Import-CSV creates objects that are like tables from the CSV items. Each column in the CSV file is a property of an object (custom) and the items on the rows are the property values. The cmdlet will work for any CSV file, even those that are generated from Export-CSV.

The Import-CSV parameters are used in specifying the delimiters for the items and the header rows for the columns or to tell Import-CSV that the delimiter to use in the current culture is the list separator.

We can also use ConvertTo-CSV and ConvertFrom-CSV to convert a CSV string to an object and vice versa. Both of these cmdlets are the same as Import-CSV and Export-CSV except that they do not deal with files.

From version 3 onwards of PowerShell, if a row entry in a CSV file header contains an empty or a null value, a header row name is inserted by default and a warning message appears. Prior to version 3, that empty value would result in the failure of the Import-CSV command. Look at the following examples:

This shows the export of a CSV file and the import of the same. We will use Get-Process to place the process on the local system and the pipeline operator to send the objects to Export-CSV, which will them export them to a file called Processes.csv on the current directory:

```
PS C:\> get-process | export-csv processes.csv
```

The next example will show Import-CSV importing processes from the Import-CSV file. The objects that result from this will be saved in the $p variable:

```
PS C:\> $p = Import-Csv processes.csv
```

And this next example shows objects that are imported into Get-Member being piped with pipe operator. The result is the process objects are now CSV:System.Diagnostic.Process objects and not the objects that Get-Process returns, which are System.Diagnostic.Process. Note that, as we haven't put an entry type into the CSV process object format files, they will not be formatted in the way that a standard process object is. If you want the objects displayed, you need to use the correct format cmdlets, such as Format-Table, Format-List, etc. or the objects must be piped into Out-GridView.

```
PS C:\> $p | get-member

TypeName: CSV:System.Diagnostics.Process
```

```
Name                    MemberType     Definition

----                    ----------     ----------

Equals                  Method         System.Boolean
Equals(Object obj)

GetHashCode             Method         System.Int32
GetHashCode()

GetType                 Method         System.Type
GetType()

ToString                Method         System.String
ToString()

BasePriority            NoteProperty System.String
BasePriority=8

Company                 NoteProperty System.String
Company=Microsoft Corporation

...

PS C:\> $p | out-gridview
```

Finally, the last example demonstrates how the delimiter parameter is used from Import-CSV and how you should export a process to a file that makes use of the colon delimiter:

```
PS C:\> get-process | export-csv processes.csv -
Delimiter :

PS C:\> $p = Import-Csv processes.csv -Delimiter :
```

When the file is imported, Import-CSV uses the delimiter parameter to indicate the delimiter type in use.

Chapter 6: How to Make PowerShell Work For You

As you have probably already gathered, learning PowerShell is going to take some time. There is a lot going on here and although it will all make sense eventually, getting to that point will take hard work, concentration, and plenty of practice. Do put the work in because PowerShell can be so beneficial to you and, once you get to working with it, you will wonder how you managed without it. This is a brief look at how you can get PowerShell working for you:

Working with Process Cmdlets

PowerShell contains several Process cmdlets that let you manage local and remote PowerShell processes and here's an overview of them:

- **Get-Process**

This cmdlet lets you get processes that on the local computer. Simply use Get-Process without any parameters and the result will be a list of processes. If you want to get certain processes, you must specify which ones by using the ID or the name of the process. Have a look at this example showing you how you would get the IDLE process:

```
PS> Get-Process -id 0
```

The return would look something like this:

```
PS> Get-Process -id 0

Handles  NPM(K)     PM(K)       WS(K) VM(M)   CPU(s)
Id ProcessName

-------  ------     -----       ----- -----   ------
-- -----------

      0       0         0          16     0
0 Idle
```

In some situations, the Get-Process cmdlet won't return any data but, by using it with a ProcessID, if there are no matches then an error will be returned. The reason for this is that, normally, a known process that is running would be retrieved but if the ID specified doesn't have a process, the most likely scenario is that the ID is not right or the process has already exited:

```
PS> Get-Process -Id 99

Get-Process: No process with process ID 99 was found.

At line:1 char:12

+ Get-Process <<<< -Id 99
```

If you want a subset of processes based on the name of the process, you must use the Name parameter that goes with Get-Process. This will take a list of multiple names, separated by a comma and will also support the use of the wildcard. This example shows how to get all the processes with a name that begins "ex":

```
PS> Get-Process -Name ex*

Handles  NPM(K)     PM(K)      WS(K) VM(M)   CPU(s)
Id ProcessName

-------  ------     -----      ----- -----   ------
-- ----------

    234       7     5572       12484   134     2.98
1684 EXCEL

    555      15     34500      12384   134   105.25
728 explorer
```

PowerShell processes are based on the class called .NET System.Diagnostic.Process and there are several System.Diagnostic.Process conventions that it must follow. The main one is that an executable process name must never have the .exe extension at the end. However, Get-Process can take multiple values for Name:

Get-Process is also able to accept several values for the Name parameter:

```
PS> Get-Process -Name PowerShell -ComputerName
```

```
localhost, Server01, Server02

Handles  NPM(K)    PM(K)       WS(K) VM(M)   CPU(s)
Id ProcessName

-------  ------    -----       ----- -----   ------
-- -----------


    258        8    29772       38636   130
3700 powershell

    398       24    75988       76800   572
5816 powershell

    605        9    30668       29800   155     7.11
3052 powershell
```

There is another Get-Process parameter you can use, called
ComputerName and this will get the processes from remote
computers. For example, the following command will get
processes from 2 remote computers and the local computer,
localhost:

```
PS> Get-Process -Name PowerShell -ComputerName
localhost, Server01, Server02

Handles  NPM(K)    PM(K)       WS(K) VM(M)   CPU(s)
Id ProcessName

-------  ------    -----       ----- -----   ------
-- -----------


    258        8    29772       38636   130
3700 powershell
```

```
    398        24      75988      76800     572
5816 powershell

    605         9      30668      29800     155      7.11
3052 powershell
```

The display doesn't show the computer names but they
inside the property called MachineName, from the processes
that Get-Process returned. Another command shows you
how to display the MachineName properties, ProcessID and
ProcessName for each Process object, using Format-Table:

```
PS> Get-Process -Name PowerShell -ComputerName
localhost, Server01, Server01 | Format-Table -
Property ID, ProcessName, MachineName

  Id ProcessName MachineName

  -- ----------- -----------

3700 powershell  Server01

3052 powershell  Server02

5816 powershell  localhost
```

The next one is somewhat more complex and it shows you
how to add a property, namely the MachineName property to
the display for Get-Process, using a continuation character,
the backtick:

```
get-process powershell -computername localhost,
Server01, Server02 | format-table -property Handles,
`
```

```
@{Label="NPM(K)";Expression={[int]($_.NPM/1024)}}, `

@{Label="PM(K)";Expression={[int]($_.PM/1024)}}, `

@{Label="WS(K)";Expression={[int]($_.WS/1024)}}, `

@{Label="VM(M)";Expression={[int]($_.VM/1MB)}}, `

            @{Label="CPU(s)";Expression={if
($_.CPU -ne $()`

            {$_.CPU.ToString("N")}}}, `

            Id, ProcessName, MachineName -
auto


Handles  NPM(K)  PM(K) WS(K) VM(M) CPU(s)  Id
ProcessName  MachineName

-------  ------  ----- ----- ----- ------  -- -------
----  -----------

   258       8 29772 38636   130         3700
powershell Server01

   398      24 75988 76800   572         5816
powershell localhost

   605       9 30668 29800   155 7.11     3052
powershell Server02
```

- **Stop-Process**

PowerShell is flexible when it comes to listing processes but sometimes you may want to stop a process. To do that you use Stop-Process, specifying the name or the ID of the process you to be stopped. Now, whether the process can be stopped will depend entirely on the permissions that your profile has and there are some processes that can't be stopped, regardless of permissions. If for example, you tried to stop the IDLE process, an error would occur:

```
PS> Stop-Process -Name Idle

Stop-Process: Process 'Idle (0)' cannot be stopped
due to the following error:

 Access is denied

At line:1 char:13

+ Stop-Process  <<<< -Name Idle
```

To force prompting you can make use of the Confirm parameter, useful when wildcards are used when you specify a process name. This is useful because, on occasion, you may accidentally match a process that you don't want to be stopped:

```
PS> Stop-Process -Name t*,e* -Confirm

Confirm

Are you sure you want to perform this action?
```

```
Performing operation "Stop-Process" on Target
"explorer (408)".

[Y] Yes   [A] Yes to All   [N] No   [L] No to All   [S]
Suspend   [?] Help

(default is "Y"):n

Confirm

Are you sure you want to perform this action?

Performing operation "Stop-Process" on Target
"taskmgr (4072)".

[Y] Yes   [A] Yes to All   [N] No   [L] No to All   [S]
Suspend   [?] Help

(default is "Y"):n
```

You can use object filtering cmdlets to carry out more complex data manipulations. Process objects have Resounding properties that will evaluate to True when they don't respond and, because of that, the following command can be used to stop applications that are no longer responding:

```
Get-Process | Where-Object -FilterScript
{$_.Responding -eq $false} | Stop-Process
```

You can use the same kind of approach in different situations. Let's suppose that a secondary notification area application runs automatically when you open another application. This might not work properly in Terminal

Services sessions but you may still require it on Physical console sessions. Any session that connects to the desktop has a session ID of 0; this means that you may stop every instance of a process in use by other sessions. We do this with the SessionID and Where-Object:

```
Get-Process -Name BadApp | Where-Object -FilterScript
{$_.SessionId -neq 0} | Stop-Process
```

The Stop-Process cmdlet does not have a ComputerName parameter so, to stop processes on remote computers, you would need to use Invoke-Command. For example, stopping the PowerShell process on a remote computer with a name of Server01 would require this command:

```
Invoke-Command -ComputerName Server01 {Stop-Process
Powershell}
```

PowerShell and WMI

WMI stands for Windows Management Instrumentation and it is the core of system admin, due to its ability to show vast amounts of information in a uniform manner. Because you can do so much with WMI, perhaps the most useful of the cmdlets is Get-WmiObject. We are going to take a brief look at how to use this cmdlet for accessing WMI objects and then using them for specific tasks.

- **Listing WMI Classes**

The very first thing you will want to figure out is what can be done with WMI. WMI contains hundreds of classes, some of them with multiple properties, and these classes describe the resources that can be managed. Get-WmiObject makes WMI discoverable and using the next command will show you all of the WMI classes present on the local computer:

```
PS> Get-WmiObject -List
```

```
__SecurityRelatedClass                    __NTLMUser9X

__PARAMETERS
__SystemSecurity

__NotifyStatus
__ExtendedStatus

Win32_PrivilegesStatus
Win32_TSNetworkAdapterSettingError

Win32_TSRemoteControlSettingError
Win32_TSEnvironmentSettingError
```

. . .

The same information can be got off a remote computer using the ComputerName parameter with a specific computer name or IP address:

```
PS> Get-WmiObject -List -ComputerName 192.168.1.29
```

```
__SystemClass                          __NAMESPACE

__Provider
__Win32Provider

__ProviderRegistration
__ObjectProviderRegistration

. . .
```

The list of classes that a remote system returns will differ depending on the operating system and what WMI installations other applications have added.

Note - using Get-WmiObject to connect to a remote computer can only be done if the remote system is running WMI. Also, you must ensure that the account you are using is included in the local administration group for the remote system – this is done through the default configuration settings. However, it is not necessary for the remote computer to have PowerShell and this means that you can administer those systems that don't have PowerShell but do have WMI.

When you connect to a local computer you can also use ComputerName, the IP address, the name of the local computer, a loopback IP address of 127.0.0. or the '.' WMI-style for the computer name. For example, if PowerShell were running on a computer with a name of Admin01, and an IP address 192.168.1.90, the following command would be required to show all the WMI classes in the system (pick one style only):

- `Get-WmiObject -List`
- `Get-WmiObject -List -ComputerName .`
- `Get-WmiObject -List -ComputerName Admin01`
- `Get-WmiObject -List -ComputerName 192.168.1.90`
- `Get-WmiObject -List -ComputerName 127.0.0.1`
- `Get-WmiObject -List -ComputerName localhost`

Get-WmiObject uses the root/cimv2 namespace but you can specify a different one by using the parameter called NameSpace, along with the corresponding namespace path:

```
PS> Get-WmiObject -List -ComputerName 192.168.1.29 -
Namespace root


__SystemClass                              __NAMESPACE

__Provider
__Win32Provider

. . .
```

Displaying WMI Class Details

Sometimes, you will know which WMI class you want to use to get access to information. One fo the most commonly used of these classes is Win_32OperatingSystem and it si used to get computer system information:

```
PS> Get-WmiObject -Class Win32_OperatingSystem -
Namespace root/cimv2 -ComputerName .



SystemDirectory : C:\WINDOWS\system32

Organization    : Global Network Solutions

BuildNumber     : 2600

RegisteredUser  : Oliver W. Jones

SerialNumber    : 12345-678-9012345-67890

Version         : 5.1.2600
```

Although we have shown all the parameters needed, we could express this in a much better way. If you are connecting to a local system, you don't need to use the ComputerName parameter; we have only shown it so that you can see how it works and so you know it is available if you need to use it. NameSpace defaults to root/cmv2 and you don't need to use that either. Finally, a high percentage of the cmdlets allow you to omit the mist common of the parameter names. For example, if you didn't give a name for the first Get-WmiObject parameter, it would be treated as the Class Parameter by PowerShell. So, you could actually forget all of the above commands and type it like this:

```
Get-WmiObject Win32_OperatingSystem
```

To see all of the properties in the Win32_OperatingSystem class, use Get-Member:

```
PS> Get-WmiObject -Class Win32_OperatingSystem -
Namespace root/cimv2 -ComputerName . | Get-Member -
MemberType Property


    TypeName:
System.Management.ManagementObject#root\cimv2\Win32_O
peratingSystem


Name                                       MemberType
Definition

----                                       ----------
----------

__CLASS                                    Property
System.String __CLASS {...

...

BootDevice                                 Property
System.String BootDevic...

BuildNumber                                Property
System.String BuildNumb...

...
```

Displaying Non-Default Properties Using Format Cmdlets

If you want to see information other than the default information in the Win_32Operatng System class, use the format cmdlets. For example, to see the memory data available, type in:

```
PS> Get-WmiObject -Class Win32_OperatingSystem -
Namespace root/cimv2 -ComputerName . | Format-Table -
Property
TotalVirtualMemorySize,TotalVisibleMemorySize,FreePhy
sicalMemory,FreeVirtualMemory,FreeSpaceInPagingFiles
```

```
TotalVirtualMemorySize TotalVisibleMem
FreePhysicalMem FreeVirtualMemory
FreeSpaceInPagingFiles
```

```
--------------- --------------- --------------- -----
---------- -------------
2097024          785904           305808
2056724          1558232
```

Note – You can use wildcards with property names in Format-Table and that helps to cut down the last element in the pipeline to:

```
Format-Table -Property TotalV&#42;,Free&#42;
```

You would probably find it easier to read the memory data as well, if you formatted it as a list:

```
PS> Get-WmiObject -Class Win32_OperatingSystem -
Namespace root/cimv2 -ComputerName . | Format-List
TotalVirtualMemorySize,TotalVisibleMemorySize,FreePhy
sicalMemory,FreeVirtualMemory,FreeSpaceInPagingFiles


TotalVirtualMemorySize  : 2097024

TotalVisibleMemorySize  : 785904

FreePhysicalMemory      : 301876

FreeVirtualMemory       : 2056724

FreeSpaceInPagingFiles  : 1556644
```

PowerShell v5

PowerShell is packed wth features and version 5.0 has seen the addition of some significant ones that vastly improve the way it can be used and gives you more comprehensive control over Windows-Based environments. Version 5.0 is backward compatible which means that the following, all designed to work in earlier versions of POWerhell will work in version 5.0:

- Providers
- Cmdlets
- Modules
- Snapins
- Functions
- Scripts
- Profiles

There is no need to perform a manual upgrade to the latest version if you already have an earlier one; simply make sure your Windows updates are performed and you will be n the new version. PowerShell itself also automatically updates.

Major Features of v5

Windows Server 2012 introduced Desired State Configuration and PowerShell 5.0 builds in it with a brand new feature called OneGet. This makes the discovery and installation of software on your computer much easier. OneGet is a module that provides easy access to all the software packages on the Chocolatey Repository. Chocolatey is a package manager for Windows, a framework that helps with the installation of applications and tools on your computer. The repository uses Powershell to deliver packages built on the NuGet infrastructure and on Visual Studio. With OneGet you can:

- List the repos for the packages that can be installed on your system
- Manage the repos
- Search and filter the repos
- Install and uninstall software from the repos using PowerShell
- Learn the OneGet command, Import-Module

There are several cmdlets that allow you to automate VLANS and Ethernet ports but, in case you are concerned, rest assured that the cmdlets can only control network switches that have passed the Certified For Windows Program.

Windows Management Framework 5.0

WMF 5.0 has PowerShell 5.0 and PowerShell ISE updates, including:

- Cmdlets for package management
- Cmdlets for network switches

Windows PowerShell Desired State Configuration (DSC)

DSC is like a function but, instead of scripting processes, Resource blocks and Bodes are specified instead. To use this, you need .NET 4.5 – do NOT use on any machines running

Exchange Server or any production machine. The operating systems supported include:

- Windows 7
- Windows 8.1
- Windows Server 2008 R2
- Windows Server 2012
- Windows Server 2012 R2

Check Your Version of PowerShell with $Host

In PowerShell 5.0, there is a command that will let you check the PowerShell version you are running:

```
# Windows PowerShell Version Check

Clear-Host

$Host

Name:                    Windows PowerShell ISE Host

Version:         5.0

InstanceId:              d36fdafd-f9e9-4642-bc85-
6dea29105f61

UI:              System.Management.Automation.


    Internal.Host.InternalHostUserInterface

CurrentCulture:    en-GB
```

```
CurrentUICulture: en-US

PrivateData:
     Microsoft.PowerShell.Host.ISE.ISEOptions

IsRunspacePushed:          False

Runspace:                  System.Management.Automation.

                           Runspaces.LocalRunspace
```

Chapter 7: PowerShell Terminology

When you start to learn PowerShell, you will come across terms and words that don't make a lot of sense. I have attempted to explain some of these as I have used them but, for the sake of ease, the most common ones are listed here with a fuller explanation of what they mean:

Cmdlet

A cmdlet, actually pronounced as Command-let, is the core unit of execution in PowerShell. They are like commands, compiled in the .NET language, usually C#. Each cmdlet follows a naming convention called VerbNoun which makes them incredibly easy to get the hang of. The verb is derived from a standard set of verbs and if you run the cmdlet Get-Verb at the prompt, you can see a list of all of them. The noun is the singular of the object you are working with. The VerbNoun convention makes it easy to see what a cmdlet is going to do. To see all cmdlets, type Get-Command at the prompt.

Alias

Like it is in real-world, an alias is simply another name, in this case, for a PowerShell command. That command may be a function, cmdlet or application. To make a custom alias, use New-Alias cmdlet. Aliases are used to simplify the amount of typing needed. For example, if you wanted to use the cmdlet Get-Service, you could just type in gsv. PowerShell contains several built-in aliases but, although they may things look a bit more streamlined, they can be confusing and somewhat cryptic so it is better practice to use the full name.

Variable

Like in any computer programming language, a variable is a storage space. They have names that are written like ComputerName but, if you want to access or reference a variable, you need to prefix the name with $. Variables are the best way of referencing values that may change, like numbers:

```
$i = 123
```

That variable can now be used in any expression in PowerShell

```
$i*2
```

The value that is in $1 can be changed and then you run the command again. Variables also hold results of commands.

```
$s = Get-Service | where {$_.status -eq 'running'}
```

The variable with the name S has got the output of the Get-Service expression, all of the services that are running. You can access the contents of $s when you want and you can use them in whatever way you like.

Provider

Providers are sometimes known as psprovider and they allow you to use commands to access different systems. You could think of it as being like an interface that switches between PowerShell and Windows. The provider is a small piece of software that translates cmdlets for use in underlying systems. For example, there are built-in providers for FileSystem and Registry, both different systems; you can use the cmdlet to navigate both of the systems. The Provider will translate the cmdlet so that you can use it in both. If you want to see all of the providers, type Get-PSProvider at the prompt.

Pipeline

The PowerShell pipeline is the most important part of
PowerShell, despite it not being a new idea and certainly not
unique to PowerShell. A pipeline is a construct that passes
objects between commands until your commands are
finished. The command needs to be designed in a way that a
pipelined input can be passed to it but, luckily, many of the
commands in PowerShell are already written in the right
way. If there are any objects remaining when the pipeline is
done, PowerShell will display them. One interesting part of
Pipelines is that it can be started with an object of one type
and ended with another type. For example, you could have
an expression like this one:

```
Get-Process | where {$_.ws -gt 100MB} | Measure-
Object -Property WS -Sum
```

At the beginning, we have a process object and, by the end of
the pipeline, we have the GenericMeasureInfo object.

Script

A script in PowerShell is a text file with the file extension
.ps1. Scripts are executed the way batch files are executed.
They are nothing more than series of commands, stored in
files. Each command is executed when the file is run, in the
order that they are written. There is no real difference

between running these command in the Shell or in a script. On occasion, you can take a command out of a script file and paste it into the console, where PowerShell will run it.

Function

A function is a small piece of code designed with a specific purpose. Functions can be very simple or they can be very complex. Some of the more complex can accept pipelined inputs, contain help, validation of parameters, and a lot more besides. Functions are similar to cmdlets in script version. They can be created in scripts without needing to use Visual Study for programming purposes.

Module

A module is a package of commands, all of which are related. Get-Module will show you all the available modules and all of those that are already loaded. However, before any of the commands inside a module can be used you must import them. Luckily, PowerShell does this automatically when a command inside it is first used.

Snapin

A Snapin or a PSSnapin as they are sometimes known is a type of command package. When PowerShell first came out, Snapins were the way in which additional commands were brought in, packaged up in a way that meant they had to be installed in the system and registered before use. These days, PowerShell has moved on and most of the extensions are delivered via modules. However, you should still know what they are so, to get a list of all the Snapins, type Get-PSSnapin at the prompt.

Conclusion

Thank you again for purchasing this book!

I hope this book was able to help you to understand PowerShell better, what it can do and how to use it to its full potential

The next step is to practice and practice hard. Increase your learning; there are plenty of tutorials on the internet and the biggest source of all is Microsoft itself, with pages of help dedicated to learning PowerShell. Don't worry if you make mistakes because you can always start over – the easiest way to learn is to make mistakes!

Finally, if you enjoyed this book, then I'd like to ask you for a favor, would you be kind enough to leave a review for this book on Amazon? It'd be greatly appreciated!

Thank you and good luck!

References

Some of the coding examples in this book are courtesy of external websites:

https://blogs.technet.microsoft.com/

https://stackoverflow.com

http://technet.microsoft.com

http://msdn.microsoft.com

Made in the USA
Lexington, KY
26 February 2018